I'M SO GLAD YOU ASKED

Four Stories for Children Living in Families with Drug and Alcohol Addictions

Patricia Newell Bennett

with Marguerite M. Sheehan

Illustrations by Kenny Lockwood

I'M SO GLAD YOU ASKED
RETIRED LOGO
1986-2010

Volume copyright ©Pondmark, Inc. 1985, 1995, 2011
Illustrations ©2011 Kenny Lockwood
Pondmark Inc.
POB 314, Chilmark, MA 02535
www.imsogladyouasked.com
Phone: 508-645-5099

Published by Vineyard Stories
Edgartown, MA 02539
508 221 2338
www.vineyardstories.com

ISBN 9780976782254
Library of Congress number 2011920789
Printed in China

FOR DILLON AND LULU
. . . and all children everywhere.
Here's to a bright future.

Table of Contents

"I'M SO GLAD YOU ASKED."

A story about *asking* before putting things in your mouth!

Written by Patricia Newell Bennett
and Marguerite M. Sheehan

Illustrated by Kenny Lockwood

"I'M SO GLAD YOU ASKED."

GROWN-UPS' PREPARATION PAGE

Packaging, flavoring, appearance and a myriad of other factors can make it impossible for adults to tell the difference between something that is safe and something that might be lethal.

For young children, with so little impulse control, it is crucial that they be encouraged always to ask if something is safe before putting it in their mouths — and that they don't need to wonder, for even a moment, whether it's OK to ask.

This lesson is a perfect example of how important it is for children (and, really, for all of us) to know that "there are no stupid questions."

QUESTIONS TO CONSIDER:

Do you put anything in your mouth that isn't good for you? Alcohol, drugs, food, etc. Most of us do – at least now and then. How does it affect you? Who else is affected?

As an adult, how often have you been tempted by the look or fragrance of something that was not safe to ingest? (Hand soaps and lotions, candles, dishwashing detergent, room deodorizers, antifreeze and medications are all culprits.)

Do you stop to ask yourself if certain things are safe for you? Do you utilize resources that are available to you if you have questions or concerns (your family doctor, local Poison Control, community services)?

Once there was a little boy named Michael, who lived with his mother, his grandpa and his dog, Spotty.

Spotty was the kind of dog that would eat anything and everything in sight, if you let her.

Michael's mom even kept the bread on top of the refrigerator so that Spotty couldn't get it and eat the whole loaf!

One day Spotty and Michael were playing stick in the yard. Spotty started sniffing under Grandpa's favorite rocking chair on the porch.

Michael ran right over and saw a bright-red thing that looked an awful lot like candy, just under the chair. He scooped it up quickly so that Spotty wouldn't eat it.

"Wow! A little hot ball," he said to himself. And it wasn't even dirty. He smelled it, and it smelled kind of sweet. It sure looked good. Michael wondered if he should eat the shiny, red, sweet thing.

He remembered that his mom and grandpa always told him not to eat anything that he found, because it might be poisonous and cause him to be sick.

Michael hated getting sick.

He remembered last summer when he had woken in the night with a terrible tummy ache.

He remembered how much he hated throwing up.

Spotty wagged and wagged her tail, as if to say, "Come on, Mike. Let's play stick!"

Michael put the shiny red thing in his pocket and ran into the barn to find Grandpa.

"Grandpa, look what I found. Can I eat it? I think it's a hot ball!" Grandpa came out of the barn, where he'd been feeding the chickens. He looked at Michael's shiny little red thing.

"Oh, Michael, *I'm so glad you asked* before you put that in your mouth. It looks and smells like a hot ball, but it's really my heart medicine.

"Remember when I went to the doctor and she told me that I needed to take medicine to help my heart get better? This is the medicine. It must have fallen out of my pillbox when I was resting this morning in my rocking chair.

"*I'm so glad you asked* because if you had eaten it you would have gotten sick for sure. Medicine might look like candy, but it isn't."

Michael looked a little sad, because he was really hoping to eat a hot ball for dessert.

Grandpa suggested that they go to the grocery store before lunch and get a good snack for Michael, Grandpa and Mom.

When Mom got home from work later in the afternoon, Michael could tell her the story of the shiny red thing.

Mom got home at snack time, and Michael did tell her what had happened.

He told her how he had kept Spotty from eating the pill, and how he had asked Grandpa before eating it himself … and how Grandpa had taught him about medicine.

Mom gave Michael a big hug and said, "I'm so proud of you. *I'm so glad you asked!*"

— THE END —

LOOK-ALIKES Candy and Common Household Medications

Young children with little or no impulse control are extremely susceptible to household medications left within reach. The purpose of this display is twofold:

First and foremost, for adults, it is a dramatic display of how attractive medications can be to children and how critical it is to make sure that all medications (prescription or over-the-counter) are kept well out of reach of little hands.

Second, it explains to children how important it is ALWAYS to ask a trusted adult before putting ANYTHING in their mouths: "Grown-up medicines are not safe for children."

CANDY	MEDICATION	CANDY	MEDICATION
1. Red cinnamon	Aspirin	11. Coated chocolate	Adult multivitamin
2. Pink sour candy	75 mg Amitriptyline (anti-depressant)	12. Pink sweet candy	1 mg Warfarin (blood thinner)
3. Green speckled jellybean	Doxazosin Mesylate (prostate medication)	13. Green jellybean	0.2 mg Digoxin (heart medication)
4. Valentine candy	200 mg Lamotrigine (anti-seizure)	14. After-coffee mint	Ethynodial Diacetate (birth control pill)
5. Pink licorice	260 mg Bismuth Subsalicylate (nausea, indigestion)	15. Red jelly bean	250 mg Acetaminophen (multi-symptom cold remedy)
6. Dark blue jellybean	4 mg Tolterodine Tartrate (urinary incontinence)	16. Pink candy button	10 mg Amitriptyline (anti-depressant)
7. White mint chewing gum	2 mg Nicotine Polacrilex (stop smoking gum)	17. Light blue jellybean	30 mg Pseudophedrine (nasal decongestant)
8. Red sour candy	100 mg Amitriptyline (anti-depressant)	18. Orange mint	Prenatal vitamin with iron
9. Pale yellow sweet candy	2 mg Loperamide Hydrochloride (anti-diarrheal)	19. White licorice	800 mg Ibuprofen (muscle relaxant)
10. White candy cigarettes	Real cigarettes (tobacco)	20. WARNING LABEL	It's there for a very good reason!

Topics: *Safety, Asking Before Putting Things in Your Mouth*

SELECTED BIBLIOGRAPHY

FOR CHILDREN:

Cooney, Nancy E. *The Blanket That Had to Go*. Putnam reprint, 1984.

Ellis Meyers, Connie. *Words to Say Outloud: A Safety Book for Children around the World*. Connie Ellis Myers Publisher, 2008.

Viorst, Judith. *Alexander and the Terrible, Horrible, No Good, Very Bad Day*. Aladdin, 1987.

Parr, Todd. *The Feelings Book*. Little Brown Publishing, 2005.

FOR ADULTS:

Kinney, Jean. *Loosening the Grip: A Handbook of Alcohol Information*. McGraw Hill, 2003.

Kuhn, Cynthia, et al. *Buzzed: The Straight Facts about the Most Used and Abused Drugs*. W.W. Norton, 2003.

Silverman, Harold. *The Pill Book: A Guide to the Most Prescribed Drugs in the United States*. Bantam Books, 2002.

Twerski, Abraham. *Substance Abusing High Achievers: Addiction as an Equal Opportunity Destroyer*. Jason Aronson, 1998.

KEYWORDS TO SEARCH ON LINE:

Children and Accidental Drug Overdose, Children and Accidental Drug Death, Home Safety, Keeping Your Home Safe for Children, Poison Prevention.

ALIKE...BUT DIFFERENT

A Story for Young Children about Peer Support
. . . and Parents Who Abuse Drugs

ALIKE, BUT DIFFERENT

GROWN-UPS' PREPARATION PAGE

This lesson addresses the issue of parents' use (or prior use) of drugs and alcohol in a way that interferes with their lives and their families' lives ... and introduces the concept of peer support.

It is important to help children to understand, not judge, parents (other adults/teens) who use alcohol or other drugs in an abusive way. Whenever possible, help them to understand that it is difficult to live with anyone suffering from a debilitating illness. Everyone living in that situation experiences feelings like anger, anxiety, fear, disappointment, confusion and hopelessness.

QUESTIONS TO CONSIDER:

Do you keep your fears and troubles to yourself? Do you share them?

Have you had the experience of sharing something difficult with a loving listener? A friend or family member, a spouse, clergy person, therapist or 12-Step group member?

When was the last time you reached out to your support system?

Everyone said they were alike, but different.
Benjamin and Shanda were best friends.

They both went to the same school, but Benjamin was
in kindergarten and Shanda was in first grade.

They both loved stories about the Wild West, dogs
that got lost but found their way home, and when the
dinosaurs ruled the earth.

Shanda read the words. Benjamin reminded her if she
skipped one.

Benjamin and Shanda both had the same favorite food, French fries, but they ate their French fries very differently.

Shanda sprinkled salt on each one and ate them with a fork. Benjamin covered his with ketchup and ate them with his hands.

Shanda said, "Ketchup is disgusting!"

After all, everyone said they were alike, but different.

Benjamin and Shanda both wore red high-top sneakers.

Benjamin always laced his tight, all the way to the top, and Shanda let the laces drag on the ground the way the big kids did!

If you saw their feet on the subway, you would always know who was who.

Benjamin and Shanda lived in the same house. Well, not exactly the same house. They both lived in apartments in different sides of the same house.

Shanda's side was pink with white trim. Benjamin's side was red with no trim.

Benjamin and Shanda talked about the same things.

Benjamin talked while sitting up straight, with his eyes looking out to the street, and Shanda talked while lying on her back with her eyes looking up at the clouds.

Shanda lived with her mom and her little sister. They had moved to this apartment in New York City from Barbados, where Shanda's grandmother still lived.

Shanda carried a picture of her grandmother in her wallet. She loved looking at the fruit on her grandmother's hat.

This is Shanda's grandmother.

Benjamin lived with his mother and father and no brothers or sisters. They had moved to their apartment from Texas, part of the Wild West, where Benjamin's grandma still lived.

Benjamin carried a picture of his grandma in his wallet, too. He loved looking at her big cowgirl hat.

Benjamin's grandma was coming to visit soon. Shanda couldn't wait to meet her. She hoped that Benjamin's grandma would wear that hat.

Both Benjamin and Shanda agreed that grandmothers are very special people. After all, everyone said that they were alike, but different.

This is Benjamin's grandmother.

They both talked about their parents.

Benjamin's father drank too much alcohol and smoked too much marijuana and cocaine. He stayed home a lot and fell asleep on the couch or got grouchy at Benjamin.

Benjamin's dad always said he would play ball with him later, but later never came.

Benjamin's mother simply worked all the time. She said, "Somebody has to pay the rent!"

Shanda's mom used to drink too much alcohol. Now she doesn't drink at all, and is always getting a babysitter for Shanda and her sister so she can go to A.A. meetings* and talk about how it feels not to drink.

She says, "Quitting isn't easy, but I'm tired of drinking."

*NOTE: For AA/NA meetings in your area:
See Alcoholics Anonymous or Narcotics Anonymous
in your local telephone directory

- or call -

Alcoholics Anonymous National Referral line at 1-800-923-8722 or
The National Alcohol and Drug Abuse Hotline at 1-800-771-6686

Benjamin was sad that his father drank too much and smoked drugs all day. He wished that his dad would read to him or play checkers instead. He wished his mom didn't work so much either.

Shanda was very happy that her mom didn't drink alcohol any more, but she wished that her mom didn't go to so many A.A. meetings. She missed her, even though the babysitter made great popcorn.

Sometimes Benjamin came over to Shanda's side of the apartment house and they ate popcorn and played with plastic dinosaurs.

You see, in many ways Benjamin and Shanda were alike, but different.

Benjamin and Shanda agreed on a lot of things.

They both liked jeans better than shorts.

They both thought that lime green was the best color for sidewalk chalk and that "ghost stories" should only be told in the daylight.

Another thing they both agreed on was, "It's absolutely important to have a best friend."

Benjamin and Shanda were best friends.

They thought that in some ways they were different,
but that mostly ... they were alike.

— THE END —

ALIKE BUT DIFFERENT

Topics: *Peer Support, Family Alcoholism, and Drug Addiction*

SELECTED BIBLIOGRAPHY

FOR CHILDREN:

Crossen, Denise. *Mommy's Gone to Treatment*. Central Recovery Press, 2008.

Hastings, Jill. *An Elephant in the Living Room*. Hazelden Press, 1984.

Parr, Todd. *The Best Friends Book*. Little Brown Books, 2005.

Willems, Mo. *Knuffle Bunny Too: The Case of Mistaken Identity*. Hyperion Books, 2007.

FOR ADULTS:

Alcoholics Anonymous. *The Big Book: The Basic Text of Alcoholics Anonymous (AA)*.
AA World Services, 1996.

Alcoholics Anonymous. *Twelve Steps Twelve Traditions*. AA World Services, 1996.

Bradshaw, John. *Homecoming: Reclaiming Your Inner Child*. Bantam, 1992.

Black, Claudia. *Straight Talk: What Recovering Parents Should Tell Their Kids about Drugs and Alcohol*.
Hazelden, 2003.

Narcotics Anonymous. *Book One: Narcotics Anonymous*. World Services Office, 1988.

Woititz, Janet. *The Complete ACOA Sourcebook of Adult Children of Alcoholics at Home, at Work, in Love*.
Health Communications, 2002.

KEYWORDS TO SEARCH ONLINE:

Addiction, Recovery, Alcohol Addiction and Recovery, Drug Addiction and Recovery, Alcohol Treatment, Drug Treatment, Alcoholics Anonymous, Narcotics Anonymous, Al-Anon, 12 Step Programs, 12 Step Recovery Programs, 12 Step Meetings.

THE TROUBLESOME TUMMY BUG

Sally had
a new school,
a new teacher,
new friends, and
a *terrible* tummy ache!

THE TROUBLESOME TUMMY BUG

GROWN-UPS' PREPARATION PAGE

This story addresses the physical effects of holding in negative emotions. Anger is a powerful emotion. Handled poorly, it produces destructive results for everyone involved. Unmanaged anger can lead to arguments, assault, physical abuse and self-harm.

Poorly managed or suppressed anger causes the presence of stress-related chemicals in the body. Over time, these chemicals can cause us harm.

Some of the health problems that have been linked to anger include: headache, digestive problems, insomnia, anxiety disorders, depression, high blood pressure, heart attack and strokes.

QUESTIONS TO CONSIDER

When you were a child, how did you express your anger?
How did the members of your family express their anger?

How do you express your anger now?
Are you comfortable with how you express your anger?
Do you need any support with expressing anger — or expressing anger in healthier ways?

Well-managed, safely expressed anger can be a useful emotion, encouraging healthy conversation and positive life changes. You and your loved ones (and your body) deserve it!

Sally was five years old.

In the morning her dad drove her to the Ross School for kindergarten.

Then, after lunch, she rode on the big yellow school bus to the after-school program at her old day care.

Dad picked her up at the end of the day on his way home from work.

It was a long day, and Sally sometimes fell asleep in the car on the way home.

Then Dad had to wake her up for supper.

One day when Dad picked her up, Sally complained that she had a tummy ache.

By the time they got home, it felt better, so Dad didn't worry too much. "We'll watch it," he said.

The next day, when it was time to go home from school, Sally had a tummy ache again. This tummy ache went away soon, too.

Every day that week, Sally had a tummy ache.

Finally Dad made a silly joke about the Troublesome Tummy Bug, and Sally started to cry.

"I hate kindergarten!" she said.

"Every time we go out for recess the other kids grab the ball, and I never get to play.

"I'm so mad! I'm going to quit kindergarten and go back to day care all day."

Dad gave Sally a big hug and said, "That must be what the Troublesome Tummy Bug is all about.

"When you are mad about something and you don't tell anyone that you're mad, your tummy starts to hurt. That can be a tummy's way of saying, 'I'm mad!'

"I'm so glad you told me about the problem at recess. I don't want you to have tummy aches, and I don't want you to miss out on playing ball.

"Tomorrow morning, let's talk to your kindergarten teacher."

The next morning, when Dad took Sally to school, he and Sally went in together.

Dad held Sally's hand while she told her teacher, Ms. Jackson, about the tummy aches and about how mad she was that she never got to play ball.

Ms. Jackson said, "Oh, Sally, I'm so glad you told me. From now on we will be sure that all the kids get a chance to play ball.

"We'll take turns, and I'm going to order some extra balls today!"

When Dad came to pick up Sally at the end of the day, she was so happy to see him.

She didn't have a tummy ache, and she was so excited that she wasn't even tired. "Ms. Jackson made sure that all the kids got turns with the ball," she said.

"I had a great day. I guess I won't quit school after all."

Dad was excited, too. "That's great, Sally."

Telling people when you are angry can sure be hard, but stomach aches hurt, too! "Talking seems to scare that Troublesome Tummy Bug away."

Sally laughed and asked, "What's for supper?"

— THE END —

TROUBLESOME TUMMY BUG

Topics: *Sharing and Addressing Difficult Feelings*

SELECTED BIBLIOGRAPHY

FOR CHILDREN:

Cain, Janan. *The Way I Feel.* Parenting Press, 2000.

Goldblatt, Rob. *The Boy Who Didn't Want to Be Sad*. Magination Press, 2004.

Miller, Ron. *I Was So Mad*. Random House, 2000.

Viorst, Judith. *Alexander and the Terrible, Horrible, No Good, Very Bad Day*. Aladdin Library, 1987.

Willems, Mo. *The Pigeon Has Feelings Too*. Hyperion Books, 2005.

FOR ADULTS:

Gray, John. *What You Feel You Can Heal: Enriching Relationships*. Heart Publishing, 1994.

Hendrix, Harville. *Getting the Love You Want: A Guide for Couples*. Owl Books, 2001.

Lerner, Harriet. *The Dance of Anger*. Harper Collins Publishing, 1997.

Woititz, Janet. *Struggle for Intimacy*. Health Communications, 1993.

KEYWORDS TO SEARCH ONLINE:

Expressing Feelings, Addressing Difficult Feelings, Identifying Feelings, Sharing Feelings, Discussing Difficult Issues with Children, Communication, Communicating Feelings, Communicating Difficult Issues with Young Children.

Grown-ups Can Make Mistakes

A Story about Families and DUI

Grown-ups Can Make Mistakes
A Story about Families and DUI

GROWN-UPS' PREPARATION PAGE

The number of drunk drivers on the road is staggering. Each year more drunk drivers are arrested than the year before. All too often, children are present at the scene of these arrests. This is a frightening experience. We feel this story is important for a number of reasons:

1. To introduce the concept of driving under the influence (DUI) as a safety issue … and help children to identify risky situations.

2. To address the fears of children whose parents do drive under the influence but haven't yet been arrested.

3. To validate feelings of children who have been in a vehicle when one of their parents was arrested.

4. To present police officers and counselors as members of a positive support system, counteracting the negative associations often found in our society.

This story has been specially developed to be effective for children from both single- and two-parent families. Children may associate the grandfather with a father, another male relative or a family friend. Children may also mention adults driving under the influence of drugs other than alcohol (story allows for discussion).

Before you deliver this lesson, we want to make it clear that we do not consider driving under the influence of alcohol or other drugs to be a "mistake." Anyone old enough to get behind the wheel of an automobile knows the danger and the law. It is not a mistake to disregard those things. It is a choice. A very poor choice.

We have used the word "mistake" in this lesson because it is a word that young children can understand … and in the context of the topic (family alcoholism and addiction), it leaves judgment out.

One sunny Saturday afternoon, Kimberly Baker and her mom were going shopping for groceries.

Both Kimberly and her mom made sure that they buckled their seat belts before driving off.

They knew that seat belts help to keep you safe.

Kimberly's mom brought a can of beer along for the ride.

Even though Mrs. Baker often drank beer while she was driving, the funny feeling in Kimberly's tummy never seemed to go away.

The funny feeling in her tummy seemed to be saying, "Drinking alcohol when you are driving isn't safe!"

Suddenly, Kimberly and her mom heard a siren and saw flashing blue lights.

Police Trooper Mike was asking Mrs. Baker to pull her car over to the side of the road.

The police trooper's job is to be sure that people are driving safely.

Trooper Mike told Mrs. Baker that he had seen her swerving on the road. He also thought that she had been driving too fast. Swerving and driving too fast are dangerous.

Trooper Mike asked her to get out of the car so he could see if she had been drinking alcohol. Troopers know that drinking alcohol can make people drive unsafely.

Trooper Mike asked Kimberly's mom to walk a straight line so he could tell if she had been affected by drinking alcohol.

Kimberly watched from the car. She could tell that her mom could not walk in a straight line. Kimberly was scared. What would happen now?

Trooper Mike told Kimberly's mom that he thought it would be best if she did not drive anymore that day.

Trooper Mike told Mrs. Baker that drinking alcohol when you are driving is against the law and that his job was to take her to the police station, where she would be safe.

Trooper Mike told Kimberly that the next part might be a little scary. He told her that everyone who drinks alcohol while driving has to wear handcuffs in the police car, even mommies.

Then Trooper Mike gave Kimberly and her mom a ride to the police station.

At the police station. Trooper Mike called Kimberly's grandpa to come to take Kimberly home.

He told her that Mrs. Baker would have to stay at the police station for the whole afternoon.

Then, after supper, Kimberly and her grandpa could come back to the police station to pick up Mom. They all waved goodbye, and Grandpa took Kimberly home.

Kimberly didn't like leaving Mommy at the police station. She cried on the way home.

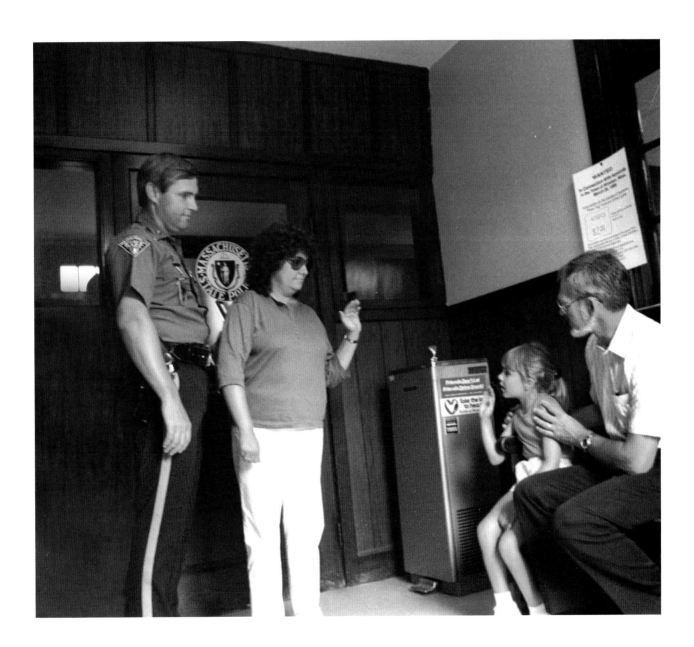

Kimberly and Grandpa spent the afternoon talking about Trooper Mike and drinking alcohol and driving.

Grandpa told Kimberly that he knew it had been scary when Trooper Mike had stopped her mommy from driving.

Grandpa explained that grown-ups sometimes make mistakes. Mommy had made a mistake by drinking beer when she was driving the car. Trooper Mike was keeping her safe.

At supper, Grandpa showed Kimberly when they could go to pick up Mommy. It was almost time.

When they got to the police station, Kimberly and her mom were so glad to see each other. Kimberly stood right next to Mom. Grandpa was there, too.

The trooper told Kimberly's mom that she could not drive her car for a few weeks. She would also have to take a class and talk to someone about drinking alcohol and driving.

On Monday morning, Grandpa and Kimberly drove Mommy to see the counselor who helps families learn about drinking alcohol and driving.

Kimberly sat on Mommy's lap. She was happy that the funny feeling in her tummy was going away.

The counselor said that everyone makes mistakes, even mommies. Kimberly laughed and said, "Grandpa told me that at home!"

Then Grandpa drove Kimberly and her mom home.

It felt so good to be sitting in the middle and to know that the whole family was learning how to be safe together.

— THE END —

GROWN-UPS CAN MAKE MISTAKES

Topics: *DUI, Criminal Behavior, Trauma*

SELECTED BIBLIOGRAPHY

FOR CHILDREN:

Hazen, Nancy. *Grown-Ups Cry Too: Los Aldultos Tambien Lloran*. Lollipop Power, 1973.

Holmes, Margaret. *A Terrible Thing Happened: A Story for Children Who Have Witnessed Violence or Trauma*. Magination Press (The American Psychological Association), 2000.

Lester, Helen. *Something Might Happen*. Houghton/Mifflin, 2003.

Simon, Norma. *Nobody's Perfect, Not Even My Mother*. Albert Whitman, 1987.

FOR ADULTS:

Brownell, Rachael. *Mommy Doesn't Drink Here Anymore: Getting Through the First Year of Sobriety*. Conari Press, 2009.

Milkman, Harvey. *Criminal Conduct and Substance Abuse Treatment: Strategies for Self-Improvement and Change, Pathways to Responsible Living*. Sage Publications, 2005.

Wanberg, Kenneth, *Driving with Care: Alcohol, Other Drugs and Driving Safety Education. Strategies for Responsible Living*: The Participant Workbook, Level 1 Education, Sage Publications Inc., 2005.

Wanberg, Kenneth, *Driving with Care: Alcohol, Other Drugs and Impaired Driving Offender Treatment— Strategies for Responsible Living*: The Participant Workbook, Level II Therapy, Sage Publications Inc., 2005.

KEYWORDS TO SEARCH ONLINE:

Drinking and Driving, Alcohol and Driving, Driving While Intoxicated, Driving High, DUI, Blood Alcohol Content, Intoxication, Legally Intoxicated, Consequences of DUI, Driver Alcohol Education, Alcohol Treatment and Recovery.

I'm So Glad You Asked Classroom/Clinical Edition in a Three-Ring Binder, with CD-ROM $195.00

> Twenty lessons (4–6 months of material) complete with weekly follow-up activities
> Grown-Ups Preparation Pages to support each lesson
> Projects, Puppet Shows, Songs and Children's Stories
> Send home/sharing component for friends and family participation
> Comprehensive resource section and bibliography
> *I'm So Glad You Asked* Four in One ~ Full Color Children's Stories (see below)
> What's Drunk, Mama? — A brochure for use with children by Al-Anon Family Groups
> On Helping Addicts — A brochure for adults by Roget Lockard, M.Ed.

Text is three hole punched and set in a sturdy three-ring binder designed for the wear and tear of daily use. Durable plastic separators between each lesson provide easy access to the material. (CD-ROM allows for convenient printing of lessons and activities for posting, coloring and sharing.)

I'm So Glad You Asked Home/Office Reference Edition in Paperback, with CD-ROM $49.95

> Twenty lessons (4–6 months of material) for children complete with weekly follow-up activities
> Grown-Ups Preparation Pages to support each lesson
> Projects, Puppet Shows, Songs and Children's Stories
> Send home/sharing component for friends and family participation
> Comprehensive resource section and bibliography

(CD-ROM allows for convenient printing of lessons and activities for posting, coloring and sharing.)

I'm So Glad You Asked Replacement CD-ROM $29.95

I'm So Glad You Asked Four in One — Full Color Children's Book $19.95

> *I'm So Glad You Asked* — A story about asking before putting things in your mouth.
> *Alike, but Different* — A story about peer support and parents who abuse drugs.
> *The Troublesome Tummy Bug* — A story about talking about and resolving difficult feelings.
> *Grown-ups Can Make Mistakes* — A story about a mother, a daughter and DUI

Four full-color children's stories in one hardcover children's book. Stories address alcoholism, addiction, and other difficult issues in accessible ways for young children. All four stories are included in black and white as part of the text of the paperback edition.

***Special ***Purchase both books and save $10 . . . . $59.95

I'm So Glad You Asked Community Curriculum Trainings — 6 Hours. $3500.00*

Design-Your-Own Full-Day Training. Choose from a variety of topics specifically suited to meet the needs of your particular community and ensure that you get just what you need to feel comfortable using *I'm So Glad You Asked* with the children and families in your care.

All trainings must include Early Childhood, Social Service, Mental and Medical Health professionals in your community. If you'd like support, we've done LOTS of these, and we'll be happy to assist you with planning. Call or email us for details. * Additional charges may apply depending on travel expenses. Minimum 20 participants. Share the cost with other programs in your area. Ten programs x $350 = $3500.